THE
DEATH OF THE
ANGRY
BLACK WOMAN

JAMELIAH YOUNG-MITCHELL

ISBN: 978-1-943258-92-5

Edited by: Jessica Carelock, Amy Ashby

Published by Warren Publishing
Charlotte, NC
www.warrenpublishing.net
Printed in the United States

*Mom, as much as I miss you, you will always be my
peace buddy, the person I call out to when I feel
like my temper is getting the best of me, the person I
give my code word. If you were alive today, I would text
you my code word to calm me down. Thank you today,
tomorrow, and forever more for being my peace buddy.*

✤CHAPTER ONE✤

THE FOUNDATION

I recall, many years ago, watching a movie called *Diary of a Mad Black Woman*. The "mad" woman in question began to illustrate and write how arguments with her husband caused her to become angry. Sure, her husband was not so nice. There are plenty of husbands out there who are great, but sometimes even great husbands mess up.

The Bible speaks about how, "It is better to live in a corner of the housetop than in a house shared with a quarrelsome wife," (Proverbs 21:9, ESV). In this verse, a man goes up to the rooftop because something has driven him up there: his wife's rage. It is the heat of her anger. It is this rage that, at some point in time, causes her husband to flee for his life, either for his own safety or to keep the peace.

I understand some men in our lives, or on television, are not so great. But believe me, they are products of their environments. Right now, I want to talk to my sisters. I want to talk about the rage and the anger, about what is making you all so unapproachable. I want to speak about what is fueling you, causing you to be rageful, bitter, and angry.

Society uses so many words to label black women. I've heard "bitter black woman," "angry black woman," and even "angry black bitch." What happened that made us embrace the title, "bitch?" And why do we publicize it's okay to call us "bitches?"

Furthermore, why is it that we accept that we can no longer be loved? Why do many respond with yelling, screaming, scratching, and clawing ourselves, each other, our families, and the men in our lives? Apparently, this is the new norm.

I am a Christian, and the Bible I read says we're "fearfully and wonderfully made," (Psalms 139:14, ESV). The Bible also speaks about how a woman is supposed to possess the "... imperishable beauty of a gentle and quiet spirit," (1st Peter 3:4, ESV). God's word about what makes a woman beautiful is different from what the world says. Having a gentle and quiet spirit doesn't mean a woman must be be a pushover or docile, but she's got to get to a place where she "dies" within her anger. She must kill the seed of her past so she can spring forth and become the beautiful flower of her future.

Perhaps your mother never taught you how to blossom in this way, but she may have taught you how to be docile and quiet. "Don't you open your mouth to your husband," she may have said. "He's the head of the house. Don't you say anything; don't you make him mad."

Some mothers react a certain way when Daddy is mad. They just sit at the table and keep their mouths shut. They prepare his meals, but know not to speak when he's angry. Despite what many of us learned as kids, it is possible to stand one's ground and be stern *without* being labeled an "angry black bitch." The secret is respect. See, the black man is not often respected, he is feared. Society puts so many labels on us and we, for some reason in our strife-filled environments, think that is acceptable. It is not.

Why is it that when I check social media or turn on the television, time and time again I see my black sisters fighting and scratching? I see them in parking lots, fighting over parking spaces. Or maybe they're at a fast-food restaurant jumping and beating on each other. There are teenage girls who have died as a result of anger. These women are angry. They're angry because maybe their dads "did not" and maybe their moms "should have." Each of these women has caused a seed to grow in her subconscious that has prevented her from becoming a healthy adult or having healthy relationships.

I remember times when I've watched things on Facebook that said black women are angry because we have to carry so much on our backs. But do we, really? I can't blame this label on the white man, because technically speaking, it isn't the "everyday" white man of today who holds us in bondage. We can no longer allow that to be an excuse.

Black women are powerful. We are powerful in the boardroom, not just the bedroom. So, why is it that we have become so comfortable pursuing someone else's husband or boyfriend and going on social media or television and boasting about how, "I took that bitch's man?" Something has happened.

It's time to bring this all to the forefront. You need to think about why, how, and when that seed was sown, and how it has sprung forth and produced the tree that is labeled "the angry black woman." It is time to call your family and friends, and talk about those things you've been holding in your subconscious. It's time to discuss those feelings that are expressed in your language, that are expressed each time you take a swing, that turn into depression and sadness, that cause your loneliness. Those negative feelings come out in so many ways because the seed of your childhood anger was never killed. Let's bring it all to the forefront. Let's begin to understand that anger.

❧CHAPTER TWO❧
LEARNING WHAT WE SEE

Children are perhaps the best recorders ever created. They can record every movie they watch, every word that is spoken. They are more powerful than the most up-to-date phone, better than the best technology on the market. They can accurately remember something profound and mimic it until it lasts a lifetime. How do they do that? They memorize by watching, hearing, practicing, and repeating. But something happens when they begin to come into their own, and it's called "choice." They begin to ask themselves, "What do I do with the knowledge I've recorded from watching my parents? What do I do with the knowledge I've received, internalized, and now make the choice to interpret?" Later, they may ask (at least in their subconscious), "How will what I've 'recorded' affect my adulthood?"

Your childhood memories are the source of your anger. Yours parents are the greatest blueprints in your life. You grew up learning to mirror them.

Those "recordings" you created as a child have helped you to make decisions in adulthood. Your anger may have begun by watching those two individuals say they were "in love."

Personally, I watched my mother become a punching bag. I recorded all those beatings, the torment she went through at my father's hands, and I realized I could not be like her. Sure, there were so many attributes about her that were beautiful. For example, she used to tell me that "a woman is what you are by nature, but a lady is what I have taught you to be." As much as I loved my mother, and watched her, and wanted to be just like her, there was a little part of her that I couldn't bring myself to replicate. Even though my eyes saw, my ears heard, and my heart gravitated toward her love, I pushed back. After all I'd witnessed in being a defender for her and my siblings—jumping up night after night to save them from beatings, or running outside without shoes to call my aunts in the next building—I made a conscious decision that, "this [was] not going to be me."

The sad thing is that so many of us watch our own mothers take beatings. Then, many of us decide to fight back. Now, each time we witness what we perceive to be that same kind of violence—whether toward ourselves, our beautiful mothers, or another loved one—we lash out. At some point, we become so tainted by our convictions that we can no longer differentiate between what is acceptable in a relationship and what isn't. The spirit of discernment is so necessary, isn't it?

Personally, I absorbed so much from my parents, it ruined my ability to see right and wrong in relationships. When I got older, I had to make a decision to do something I think my mom struggled with: I had to learn to love myself—and her. Even though she loved her children and gave us everything, she also loved her man so much she depleted her mind, body, and soul for him. In my mother, I saw a woman love a man beyond herself and give more than you could have imagined. Unfortunately, she did this at the sacrifice of her children.

Even though I loved my dad, I didn't like the way he treated my mother, so I made the conscious decision that I would not tolerate any man treating me the wrong way. As a result, for years if anyone looked at me wrong, said something wrong, smelled wrong, or raised their voice, it caused my skin to shriek. That person had hell to pay.

When women witness abuse as children, we use that abuse as our blueprint and we put plans forth. These plans are like escape plans or "what ifs." We develop a strong sense of self and we build defense mechanisms. We build up these defense mechanisms for our entire lives and, therefore, some of us don't have a snowball's chance in hell when it comes to relationships. Our defenses have desensitized us toward emotions we need to succeed, and we are programmed to come on strong in areas where maybe we don't need to fight as hard.

I want you to find a quiet place and think about what you recorded as a child and how those memories affect your decisions today. Whether we realize it or not, many of us tend to sabotage relationships because the mere thought of them makes us want to run away. Given all you may or may not have witnessed as a child, do you choose to run toward love or run away from it? Whatever you decide, that's on you.

Have you ever had a cut and the scar began to heal, but you walk by something that hits it and it begins to bleed again? That's what happens when you're programmed as a child. Your wounds heal until you hit and reopen them. It's the same with relationships. Perhaps you become involved in a relationship and someone uses certain "trigger words." Perhaps your emotional wounds are reopened anytime someone tells you to "Shut up." You might say, "Excuse me, what? Who are you talking to?" Or maybe you hit those wounds when you get involved with someone who seems a little too controlling. These "triggers" may look like the abuse (emotional or physical) you grew up with—they're familiar to you. You've already recorded and mastered every hurtful mechanism and labeled it as "unhealthy." But if you don't learn to respond appropriately to the "unhealthy" tendencies of others, you may become a raging force.

When anger takes its presence in your life, you begin to let it lead everything because that is how you survive. You begin to fight when you shouldn't. You fight mentally, you fight physically, and you try to stay two steps ahead because maybe your own mother fell so far behind. Those little eyes that recorded every fight, every beating, every bruise, developed a sense of survival within you and you have become a raging lion. And now when you sense that danger in adulthood, *everybody's* in trouble. You pounce.

When we project anger for one person onto someone else, that anger is "misplaced." But to you it doesn't feel misplaced, it feels justified. And it's targeted toward anyone who thinks they're going to come into your life and run you over. Unfortunately, this misplaced anger often manifests itself in uncontrollable behavior as you try to catch the rain before it falls. You tire yourself out. So, even though you tried to create a barrier around yourself that nobody else could penetrate, you wind up getting hurt.

All that hurt stems from the fact that your young eyes recorded when they should have looked away.

But as a child, how do you look away when you hear the screaming, the scratching, the yelling, the struggle? You can't. Especially if you're put in the position where you have to protect. *My* eyes saw and my ears heard. But now as an adult, I realize that my mother's marriage was not like my own and that her husband (my father) was not who I would have chosen.

Sometimes we need to take a step back, find a quiet place, and remind ourselves, "This anger was not my choice. However, when I allow what I recorded, witnessed, and heard as a child to follow me into adulthood, I *have* made a choice to ruin my chance at love." Allow yourself to push pause and stop the recording. You have to delete what you've been programmed to see, feel, and react to. The people you interact with everyday didn't cause the hurt you feel; you did when you chose to internalize it.

❧CHAPTER THREE❧
A MADE-UP MIND

As a young teenager, I moved to Clinton Avenue in Brooklyn, and it was at that point in my life I began to grow out of my childhood. By that point, I had learned to protect my mother. As a child, sleep for me was always short-lived. When you become your mother's protector at such a young age, sleep becomes a thing of the past.

At night, my father slept in the front room and my mother slept in the bedroom in the back; they didn't sleep together. In the room where I slept, there were three of us girls and we would always laugh together. Laughter was the only thing we had to mask our pain and make ourselves feel better. But in the middle of the night while my siblings would sleep, I wouldn't. Instead, I would worry. As my mother and siblings' guardian, I would listen for my father's footsteps. As soon as I'd hear them, I'd know something was about to go down.

Whenever trouble was brewing, I knew it wasn't because my mother had actually done anything. You see, my mother was very docile. She was quiet and humble, but she was also a powerful woman of God. My mother had a spiritual gift that allowed her to see things prophetically. Some people might have called her a psychic, but she wasn't. She was a prophet.

To this day, I believe my father was jealous of my mother's gifts. People gathered around her for her words of wisdom and courage. Who knew their responses would have such a harmful effect? My father was a pastor, and yet, my mother drew the crowds—and he did not like that.

Not only did I feel the need to shield my mother and my siblings, I also felt obligated to fill the void left by my mother's pacifism. This affected my character. Many women don't realize that when you in stay in relationship that has become abusive, you can put your children in a position where they feel like they need to be your protectors. You sign them up for a position they don't feel qualified for, but they do it anyway because they want their mommies or daddies to be safe. When I became my mother's protector, I became something my father despised; I began to fight back.

I remember lying in bed one time, when I heard my father walking. He wore a size thirteen shoe and I could always hear his footsteps going up and down the hall. I would listen for the creaks of the wooden floor—they were like an alarm system. When I'd hear those creaks, I would stick my head out the door where I could see into my parents' bedrooms. On that particular night, I climbed down from the top bunk bed and snuck into the hallway. As I crawled down the hall, I could hear my father. My mother was on the bed, and I heard my father jump on top of her and begin choking her. I could hear her gasping for air. At that moment, I threw on my cape and said, "Daddy, no!" He walked away.

I recall another time when he beat my mother and I tried to defend her; he punched me in the jaw. As a result, I still have TMJ and my jaw clicks whenever I give a kiss or chew something.

As I grew into my defender role, my personality became cold. I had made up my mind and made the conscious decision to not be like my mother. And, as a result, I became angry. Anger surfaced in my relationships and in how I responded to the mere thought of being disrespected. It was like everyone had a scarlet letter on their heads, and I made the world pay for the pain my father caused.

CHAPTER FOUR
THE DISCOVERY

Many women I come across, whether it be on social media, on television, or walking down the street, seem to have so much anger. I've spoken to tons of women from around the world who have said, "I have anger issues" or "I am so angry." A lot of these women don't understand where their anger came from. I hear countless stories—maybe they have a bit of a financial struggle, or daddy issues, or they've been abandoned—but all of these women have one issue in common: their relationships.

Relationships can be very difficult. As I mentioned in chapter two, we record or remember relationships we witnessed as children, and what we learn as kids affects how we handle relationships as adults. Many of us have made the decision that we are not going to be like our dads or our moms; we are going to be better. But even if we are better in some situations, we might be worse in others. Personally, even though I made a conscious decision to not be like my mother, I brought some of her relationship into my own personal relationships.

Proverbs 31:26 says that a virtuous woman "opens her mouth with wisdom, and the teaching of kindness is on her tongue," (ESV). When I got married, I made sure I took care of my husband and my household and I tried my best to speak words of kindness. But I had brought into my marriage anger that had nothing to do with the relationship I was building. In fact, many of my adult relationships began to remind me of the toxic environment I'd grown up in.

If you grew up in a home with abuse, or with a mother who was docile, you may have decided you weren't going to be like her. Maybe you decided that instead of taking a beating, you were going to let yourself get angry, put up your dukes, and say, "Let's rock out together." You may not realize it, but as a result of your past, you have become sensitive. Your senses have become so heightened, you have begun to interpret other people's actions and words differently.

When you have anger issues that developed as a result of your past, whether they were caused by your mother or father or somebody else, and someone uses a certain tone with you, you may find yourself reacting to "trigger words." If your dad was very mean and someone asks, in a harsh voice, "What are you looking at?" it can strike a chord. Maybe their words remind you of how your dad used to speak to your mom. Or perhaps one of your parents demanded a particular amount of order and everything had to be done their way. If you then interact with someone who wants things done a certain way, you may feel like you're being controlled. Or maybe you were abused as a child—be it physically, emotionally, or verbally. If you later meet someone who displays even a hint of what you witnessed as a child, you may immediately jump to being defensive. You may think, "Mama took that, but I'm not going to."

When you are so used to having to defend yourself and others, you fight back. If someone cuts you off in the parking lot, you say, "I'm not taking that." If someone says, "Good morning," and their tone is off-putting, you might not know how to differentiate between a tone and a disposition. And you may never learn to discern the difference if you are always looking for that "anger language" you've programmed yourself to pick up on.

As an example, perhaps a woman was involved with a man who abused her. Down the line, if she starts seeing another man, she might be afraid to disagree with him because maybe she is reminded of fights with her ex. On the other hand, a woman who grew up in a healthy household may feel peaceful at all times. She may interpret any harshness as water under the bridge—and that's fine. Your response to harshness—be it real or perceived—will be very different if you grew up in a house of strife and anger. You become immune to peace, and are instead programmed to fight back when you sense strife. As a result, everything becomes an issue.

Many of us find ourselves attracted to the same kinds of personalities we grew up with, even if they are negative. We tell ourselves we can handle it, when, truth be told, we can't. We say, "I can deal with this. I dealt with this when I was small. I'm used to this." But no, you can't, and no, you're not.

Many women wind up single because they're still dealing with their anger by saying, "I ain't gonna be like my mother. No way, nuh-uh." The truth is, there is someone out there who wants to love you through it all—but you have to love yourself first. When you forgive yourself, or forgive *them* (your father, your mother—whoever hurt you), you *free* yourself and realize you deserve to be loved. After you decide to love yourself first, when a person comes along who does not allow you to do so, you won't want to give them the time of day. But because you cannot yet identify with loving yourself and you *can* identify with strife and anger, you attract those who cause strife and anger. To you, anger is easy. You're familiar with strife.

Now let me ask you, how can we get free from anger if we can't accept that it's a problem? That's why you're here, right? Maybe you're ready to experience that "mic-drop moment" of reality and truth that makes you shout, "Oh! It takes two people to fight! I'm finally going to put my boxing gloves down." You need to accept that even though you've decided not to be like your mom (or whoever may have negatively affected your past), you're still fighting her fight in your own way.

That must stop today. That embracing of anger stops right now and you're going on a different path. It's time to take a path to find yourself. You're going to find who God created you to be: a reflection of Himself. From now on, you will look at each person you meet, and if you don't see God's reflection, you will send them on their way.

It's time to pull up the roots and kill those old seeds of negativity to find out who you really are. It's time to discover who you are without the fighting, and without the strife. Let's discover your new identity without blowing fists or vulgar language. Let's discover your real personality now that we've found the seed of your anger. Let's kill that bitter old seed. Then, once you discover who you truly are, it will be time to reintroduce yourself.

Something has been hurting you for all these years and it has made you so angry. Today, it's time to acknowledge what that something is. Let's find "you" again and rediscover life through a new set of eyes.

CHAPTER FIVE
THE PATHFINDER

As I grew up, I had more independence. Dad realized his kids were older and that everybody had moved out. My oldest siblings went to college and got their own apartments, yet I stayed close by. And while I stayed close by, I witnessed so much that is still unspoken in our family. Everyone else moving out had made my father even less restrained than before. My mother began to care for my father's illegitimate son who had showed up at the front door with his bags. Most women would have turned him away; this young man was a product of my father's infidelity, yet my mother, being who she was, made my brother's old bedroom this child's new room. She cared for this teenager as he struggled to find his way and his identity. And through that, my mother grew old and tired.

Nobody would have blamed her for giving up, but I'm so glad she didn't. By the time my half-brother moved in, I had gotten married and moved a few miles away. As a child, I'd made a decision that I would not leave home until I felt like there was a level of safety for my mother—or until I married. And so, I married.

I can remember trying on my wedding dress and being so happy to wear that dress, even though I was not really happy with marrying. I realized later that I had married to escape the madness of my parents' home.

It was during my transition of becoming a wife and then a mother that my half-brother entered our lives. I visited my mother every day to make sure she was okay, and I watched how she endured the hardship of raising another woman's son. This enraged me. At this point, my father had stopped seeing my half-brother's mother, and had taken up with another woman while leaving his son at home with my mother. My rage continued to build.

Even though my mother did not agree with what my dad did or how he treated her, because she loved him, she stayed. For a time, his abuse became financial as well as physical. She would ask him for money and he would throw two pennies at her. Eventually, she'd had enough and decided to go back to work. My half-brother was an extra mouth to feed, and she needed to find financial independence. She went back to working in the school system as a teacher.

When my mother went back to work, it made my father back up a little, and I thank God he did.

But when he backed up, he eventually backed up completely. He took several trips to Ghana and my mother was left to fend for herself. She did well, I never doubted her ability. At some point, she had to find the strength within herself. My mother's discovery of her own strength was a pivotal moment for me.

As I transitioned into adulthood, my mind began to process what my eyes had recorded as a child. I remember waking up one day and saying to myself, "When I said I'd beat a man's ass if he ever even thought about lifting lift his hand for anything but to hug me, eat, or piss, I was serious." You see, when you choose a path, your subconscious receives it.

Oftentimes you hear about women who were beaten. This was very common in the 70s when I was growing up. Many women who are beaten feel like step stools that are programmed to be perfect and suffer in silence. As a result, their girls learn this behavior. Those young women must then make a choice to either mirror or refuse their mothers' behavior. I made a choice to refuse.

When I had my beautiful daughter and later, my wonderful son, I had become so "strong," I began to realize my tough skin and my anger were unhealthy. You see, having children was the key to accepting and reversing my anger. I could not allow my children's eyes to record unhealthy behavior that in the long run would hurt their development into healthy adults. I did not want to be responsible for them learning negative behavior from my pain and anger.

When you witness behavior you know is unhealthy, you make a choice (sometimes subconsciously) of who you're going to be. In my case, I became what I'd witnessed—angry, confrontational, fearful—and it was fierce. I was married and it was not a happy marriage; it ended in divorce.

When you make the decision to be fierce, you must be very careful of the kinds of personalities you choose to blend with. If you marry a person whose personality reminds you of the abuse or turmoil you grew up with, it may strike a match and ignite a fire. In my naive eyes, when I chose to marry my first husband, this was all okay; after all, I'd chosen a fire that was already lit and I thought I was strong enough to put it out. Unfortunately, his personality just fanned the flames that were already lying dormant. If we are to build lasting relationships, we must be careful of which personality types we associate with. We mustn't fan the flame.

❧CHAPTER SIX❧

THE FIRE

A small kindling of anger that ignites with the wrong person can cause a fire.

After you are married and have laid the foundation of your relationship, if you have made the choice to hold on to anger, you walk around with a burning fire inside you. That fire is a defense mechanism that can present itself in a number of different ways. Maybe you lash out with a smart mouth; maybe it's sarcasm, cussing, or even revenge. When something triggers your defense mechanism, your survival instincts kick in. Not only do you feel a constant need to just survive, but you might become overly sensitive in areas where people who grew up in healthy environments are better equipped to cope.

Many of my black sisters grew up in environments that were so turbulent, their senses became heightened. Just like in my own experience, they saw unhealthy behavior that trickled into their adulthood. That same unhealthy behavior creates in so many women a personality that is aggressive and controlling; it strikes a match and ignites a fire of familiarity. Then, when they go on to become young adults and mothers, they become their own defenders—just like when they were young, they feel the need to protect. Now that they no longer have to protect their mothers or siblings, for instance, they master the skill of protecting themselves and their marriage. This can affect how they interact with men in general, or anyone they meet. If a certain behavior or phrase feels familiar to them, and they know in their heart of hearts that it's unhealthy, they may become defensive.

A friend of mine put it well when he said, "Even a helpless little rabbit becomes defensive when it is backed up against a wall." When you've witnessed unhealthy behavior and begin a relationship with a man who is aggressive, you may flinch when that man says the wrong things. You may even want to jump up and grab him by the jugular when he's rude or nasty, because your senses have become heightened. Your survival mode and your protective ability have become uncontrollable. The unhealthy behavior just feels normal to you. I call this "learned behavior," the church calls it a "generational curse," and society calls it "misplaced anger." Whatever you call it, this mental programming means that you will not tolerate certain behavior when you encounter it.

In marriage and in dating, you must be mindful of the kind of personality you need in a mate to help you flourish and maintain a healthy relationship. Now remarried, I have a healthy marriage, but it took time, learning, and the realization that not everybody is so mindful. And that's the problem. You have to realize that the pain you're dealing with has nothing to do with your husband or mate, but rather the foundation you built on rage. You have to learn to interact with your husband and kids, those folks who live with you in the house that rage built. That rage didn't come from them, it came from your family when you were just a child, before your husband and kids came into your life.

Now don't go blaming yourself for every issue that arises, but do be careful of the personalities you let into your house. What type of personality do you best interact with? This is where the journey gets a little misty eyed, but I have to tell you the truth.

❦CHAPTER SEVEN❦

UNCOVERING THE FOUNDATION

My foundation was brick-laid through watching someone I loved be abused. My mother wasn't running around in the streets, she was very faithful. My father, on the other hand, had a girlfriend for twenty-two years of a thirty-seven-year marriage. Everything I witnessed would later be applied to my life, so I unwittingly made a blueprint. Then, bit by bit, I began to lay the bricks of my foundation: there was a brick of abuse, there was a brick of rage, there was a brick of control, there was a brick of molestation, and so on. There were many bricks laid on my foundation. This foundation that I built would create a concrete house of anger.

It's time to take a look at the foundation upon which your bricks are laid. Through every chapter of this book, we are going to look at your foundation and crack and shatter the hateful house that was built. Keep in mind that because this is your own "house," the people you love have to live in it. Over time, growing up in a toxic environment causes a person to become sensitive until everything about someone, from their tone to their attitude, can become a trigger.

I want you to understand your own foundation, so here's an exercise: take a moment and think about the foundation that was laid in your life. You need to understand that your house was built based on what your young eyes watched. Over time, you formulated an opinion—a blueprint— through which your character evolved, and you made rules for your life. Now, in your adulthood, you still follow the rules you set during your formative years. You put those rules way back in your subconscious and now you have become reactionary and you don't even know it. That is the power of laying a foundation; your foundation produced the house in which you now dwell. So think about it: what bricks built your foundation and how can you begin to topple them?

೬CHAPTER EIGHT೬
BEAUTY IS IN THE EYE
OF THE BEHOLDER

Have you ever heard the expression "smoke and mirrors?" When you get involved with a person who is very handsome or beautiful, it's easy to receive them. Sometimes your emotions get in the way, especially as a woman, because women are emotionally driven. When you're in a relationship and you like the way you feel or the way your partner is treating you, you may relax a bit, letting go of your defense mechanism. You may let your guard down, because you want people to enjoy being with you or living with you. For many of us, a happy life involves finding someone to love and having a healthy relationship with them, but we all know this isn't always the case. So, when you finally find someone, you may look at them through rose-colored glasses.

Beauty is in the eye of the beholder. So, maybe you beheld what was before you, and you liked it, and you decided to put a ring on it and get married. But what if you then encountered a personality that caused issues?

It's time to sit down and think about the issues in others that cause you to become unhappy or cause you to react with anger. I want you to find a quiet place and take time to think through this, but first, I'll give a few examples that hit home with me. I know I don't work well with control freaks, people who are mean, or people who are rude—I don't even like rude children. I don't work well with people who are selfish and inconsiderate or people who like to debate or fight. On the other hand, I do like peacemakers. I love nurturers. Think about it: what kind of personality attracts you and do you most wish to behold?

The way you respond to people can work one of two ways. First, you can accept and mirror. Perhaps you grew up thinking the abuse or emotional issues your parents dealt with were normal, embraced them, and allowed them to remain in your life into adulthood because you were familiar with them. In reality, however, you won't know how to handle those issues as an adult. After all, your mother didn't know how to handle the abuse, nor did your dad. You were unequipped to handle their problems, because they weren't yours.

The second way to respond is to run. Many men take flight due to a lack of tools needed to build a healthy relationship. Women often run as well because they are afraid to take a chance on living beyond the walls they build to protect their hearts and feelings.

If you grew up in a household where there was abuse, you probably learned to run. So, when you find yourself in a healthy, happy relationship, you may sabotage it because you're used to running. Or maybe you were taught to fight, because your mother or father was abused and you had to protect them. Or perhaps you learned how to snap back, since your parents were always rude, even in very polite situations. Then, when someone comes along who is happy, healthy, and whole, you don't know how to deal with it.

In my opinion, this all goes back to what Mike Tyson once said: "Everyone has a plan until they get punched in the mouth." When someone who once seemed so beautiful to you becomes rude or nasty, or even punches you in the face, you react the way you learned to as a child—you become a fighter. You become a person who jumps across the table.

In our society exists a generation of women— let's say between the ages of thirteen and forty-five—who just want to fight. Back in my mother's generation, in the fifties and sixties, women fought in their own way—by being very quiet.

Their silent "fights" protected their families. As a result, here we are.

Wouldn't it be nice if we could spot people's invisible pain like red flags? Unfortunately, we don't have that ability. Instead, we have a whole lot of anger in us; we're lost, scared, and have no idea what do because we were never taught how to handle adversity. As mothers, sisters, wives, and lovers, we need to learn to tame that anger. The only way to do that is to confront the truth. And how do you confront the truth? You go way back to the root so you can begin to understand the fruit.

❧CHAPTER NINE❧

SEED, TREE, AND FRUIT

Have you ever gone to the grocery store to buy an apple or a pear, anything that grows on a tree? You instantly know exactly what you're going for; you can identify the fruit by the smell, the color, and the taste. But would you buy a pear from an apple tree or an apple from a pear tree? Although they may look somewhat similar, they are totally different. Well, it's the same way with people as we mature. You are a product of the seed from which you grew and your roots will forever connect you to your upbringing.

Some women are so viciously angry due to the seed of anger that was planted and grew into the violence they now exude. The seed developed through witnessing violence and maybe staying quiet about it. If that seed grew deep down in your soul and heart, I'm going to help you bring it to the surface.

I often tell my children, "Mommy is going to tell you the hard truth, because someone else is going to come along and tell you a soft lie." So,

here's the truth: that seed was ｣
subconscious, deep down within
it has sprung forth a root of ra╷
then becomes the tree and your br
needed to nurture the seed. You in turn produce
a bitter fruit of violence, and now society deems
you as violent, because that stubborn seed was
never killed. It buried itself in your subconscious
and was never dealt with.

Now, when you engage in a relationship and
somebody speaks to you in a way that triggers
you, that bitter fruit grows. When you go out and
someone says the wrong thing, that fruit grows.

All over the world, women bear violent fruit,
because seeds were planted in their subconscious
the moment their eyes began to witness violence
as a child. That's when *your* seed began to plant
itself in your subconscious too. Now, when a
man comes into your life, maybe he shakes the
tree a little bit. Maybe somebody at the grocery
store shakes the tree a little bit. Regardless of
who does it, when someone shakes your tree, it
causes angry fruit to fall.

All this fighting is what society calls "drama."
And since we live in a drama-driven world, we
can turn on the television and see every show
imaginable about angry, fighting women. Or
take social media; how often do we see videos of
raging young women leaping across tables until
men can't even speak to them and say hello?

See, the funny thing about these seeds of violence is that they were planted so long ago, nobody pays them any attention. We just take the label of "angry black woman" or accept it when someone says, "she's just mad." But we're not "just mad." We are hurting. We are trees that bear violent fruit due to the seeds of violence that were planted and the roots of anger that took hold. That anger has robbed us of becoming beautiful trees of life. We're no longer looked on as beautiful apple trees or pear trees, or wonderful orange trees. We're labeled as trees nobody wants to deal with. People just walk on by like we're evil. People know that if they take a bite of our violent, angry fruit, it won't go well.

In a conference one time I heard Louis Farrakhan say, "Where there are no good women, there will never be any good men." It can be argued that the angry black woman has taken her place in society, and is, to a degree, responsible for the negative stereotypes the surround black men. It is time for the angry black woman to let go of her anger, sing her own praises, and create a mental funeral home for that angry seed. It is time for the angry black woman to bury the label that was put on her.

It is time for her to die.

≋CHAPTER TEN≋
THE LIGHTBULB MOMENT

Have you ever had a moment where something became revelatory or, as I like to say, a mic-drop moment where things become clear? A eureka moment, the lightbulb turns on, *bing!* There it is! I'm talking about one of those moments when you realize what everything is about. The *why* of it all drops into your spirit and you finally understand. It feels good, doesn't it?

Anger is a simple thing when you have become accustomed to it. Today it seems like it's the new norm. Maybe you've tried to weave a blanket of security around yourself only to realize that blanket was made of anger. Psychologically, it's normal to use anger as a security blanket. But anger is a reaction to pain. Aha! Lightbulb moment.

When you harbor anger and hold onto it for a long time, it festers and it becomes rage. Rage is deeper than anger—anger smolders, but rage seeks revenge. With pain and anger at the forefront of all your confrontations, you may react with lashing out and sometimes even violence. If that pain ran deep and messed up the very core of who you were, even the slightest drop of a bucket can cause a downpour. Any new adversity that reminds you of something you've already dealt with or are still dealing with can peel the scab off a wound that was trying to heal, and you become like Paul, existing with a thorn in your side. With time and focus, however, your reaction can be controlled. Then, if you are reminded of the things that caused you pain in the past, your reaction might not be as quick. It's time to let go of that blanket.

Have you taken your blanket off? Good. It's time for your eureka, lightbulb moment where you realize that everything you need is inside of you. You have been hurting yourself by holding onto things you may or may not have the ability to fix.

Hurt people tend to hurt people. It's a vicious cycle of anger. Maybe someone in your past didn't know how to love, so they didn't love you. Or someone else was betrayed, so they betrayed you. Some of us, even in childhood, got caught in the crossfires of anger. In writing this book, I had my own breakthrough moment where I realized the anger in my childhood home wasn't about me or my siblings, we simply got caught up in the crossfires of someone else's pain.

In order to heal, you've got to grab the blanket called "anger" and remove it. But we're not going to put that blanket in a drawer. I don't want you to do that. Instead, I want you to take that blanket, get you a good pair of scissors, and cut it up. Get rid of it. I don't want you to get caught up in that vicious cycle of hurting people again. I don't want you to stop yourself from loving or having friends, or being seen as happy or even beautiful. I want you to take that security blanket off, and realize the pain you've felt is just someone else's issues causing you to hurt others. Remember: hurt people hurt people.

I always say, "You gotta do what you gotta do, until you can get where you gotta get." In this case, to get where you want to get, you have to *heal*. I hope your lightbulb has gone off and you realize now, it ain't about you. What *is* about you is how you respond and react, and so you must choose—because it *is* a choice—to be happy. Every time you display anger, the person who hurt you wins. You can't give them that power any longer. So, relinquish it today. I want you to get rid of it so you will no longer be labeled "angry." That, my dear, is the greatest gift you can give yourself: the ability to forgive, heal, and be happy.

CHAPTER ELEVEN
THE REINTRODUCTION

So, now we know where all the anger came from. We've acknowledged that it hurts and we've uncovered where the seed was planted. We've unmasked who we really are, and we've accepted that it's okay to be that person. The truth of the matter is, everybody's a little angry. What we need to avoid is over-the-top anger.

I remember one time I was doing a sip and talk where a young lady said she was so angry and felt out of control. She was so filled with rage that her husband had begun to complain about her anger issues. I met another woman who was my favorite. She said, "I had a good man and I used to just beat him up, Jameliah. I would just beat on him. He would not dare lift his hand back up to me. It's not that he was a punk or a wimp, he just refused to fight me back." She was my favorite because she was accountable for her actions and sought help. Her husband had dealt with her anger for so many years, but she couldn't understand that there was a cause and effect. She figured the problem was with him; after all, even when she was angry and lashed out, he never fought back. She had become so accustomed to fighting, and he never raised a hand toward her. I respect him. The saddest thing about the situation is that her husband finally got tired and left. Oftentimes we talk about men being the abusers, but how many men are abused by angry women and it is never spoken about?

I don't understand why some women decide they can match men in the ring. It's not possible. We were not designed that way. Bless the man who does not fight back.

I'm not saying women cause all the issues. There are some women who don't understand how they became so angry, and they may have questions, such as: How can I stop being so angry? Why have I accepted my own violence and that of others for so many years? Who is able to stand up to me and still have his dignity, his manhood?

Some women say men deserve the abuse. Not all men, just some of them. I understand. I swung a time or two myself when I did not appreciate the disrespect. But then I discovered myself. I killed the seed of anger, little by little. To do this, I had to detoxify myself—mind, body, and soul. The Bible says, "... be transformed by the renewal of your mind ..." (Romans 12:2; ESV). I renewed my mind by finding God's will for my life. That started with killing the seed that was planted inside me long ago. It had become a fruit of anger that overrode everything else.

In the past, I could be talking to someone and that seed would interfere with how I heard and processed our conversation. Instead of that person's voice, I'd hear my Dad's, even after his death. The wounds of my past had never healed. My anger came out more and more during disagreements, no matter who they were with. It was that seed that was planted in my heart, brain, and soul that now expressed itself through my voice and my eyes until I had evolved into a tree of rage.

One of the wonderful things about life is that it's full of second chances. Now that you've dug up the seed and acknowledged the truth, can you swallow it? Truth really is the hardest pill to swallow. Some people mask truth with something soft so it can be digested, but I'm not that kind of person. I believe in the hard truth. So here it is: Stop fighting. Put your hands down. Stop swinging.

You should never be in a relationship where you have to fight, and you should never be placed in a position where you have to defend yourself. Maybe you've had to be defensive for years. Maybe you've defended yourself by saying things like, "You are not going to;" "You better not;" "I wish a nigger would;" or "Bring it."

When you discover who you are, you will no longer allow people to disrespect you. You *will* talk to them about the issues you have with their approach so you can fix the problem. You will learn to use wisdom and discernment. The Bible says, in Proverbs 4, to "get wisdom." Even though it's hard to do, you need to do it for yourself. Relationships where there is violence will always end poorly, no matter who threw the first blow or said the first insult.

There's a prayer that I pray about covering your gates—your ear gates, your eye gates, your nose gate, your mouth gate. So, let's pray. Pray that the Lord covers these "gates" and uses faith to protect you in every way from the things you are exposed to. Pray for your head, saying, "God, guard my thoughts." Pray for your chest, saying, "Give me the breastplate of righteousness, so that I won't react to anger." Anger doesn't lead you anywhere but to being confused and asking yourself, "Why did I do that? I could've walked away."

Men used to be the ones who stepped out toward confrontation while women walked out, but now women are running to fight. The roles have shifted, in more ways than one. My wonderful sisters of Zion, take your place back, walk out if you need to, but find your strength. Find it. The only way to discover your strength is to rediscover who you are all over again and

focus on who you are about to become. Then—
become that!

Fighting doesn't get you anywhere, it really
doesn't. I understand someone made you mad,
but you know what? How you handle it will not
only please you, it will please God too.

The outcome is so much greater when you
finally kill the root. And, guess what? You don't
have to react in anger. You can walk away with
your dignity and with your head held high. You
can feel proud of yourself. You can feel a great
accomplishment. You'll no longer hear those
voices, and you'll walk away saying, "I did
not even break a nail!" You'll walk away with
everything intact and won't have to look back to
see if you can gather up the hair or braids that
you just snatched out from the person who made
you mad. You won't wind up on social media
fighting, scratching, and out of control. You will
no longer be that individual.

Now that you know you are fearfully and
wonderfully made, it is time to reintroduce
yourself. You are new. You are beautiful. You
are not the pain of your past, and you will no
longer allow it to dictate your future. You're
going to forgive what has been holding you
back, and you're going to realize you cannot be
held accountable for someone else's pain; it had
nothing to do with you.

Forgive yourself. Forgive everyone else. Free yourself to live and love. Free yourself to laugh. You've played a great game of hide and go seek with anger, but now you have pulled off the mask and said, "There you are. I know where you came from, and now I see my true self. Now that I've revealed who I am, I can stand here and say I am no longer lost. Unforgiveness has no strings on me. I don't have to throw a blow. I don't have to do anything that degrades my femininity. My sexy. My power. My strength. I am strong. I will let others know what they will not do in a tone that is pleasing to the most high God and is satisfactory to my soul. Nobody will disrespect me."

It's time to pick your head up and walk out the door, realizing you have shaken the soil from your feet and moved on.

CHAPTER TWELVE
THE BEAUTIFUL MONSTER

Today you must choose to die of your old ways. You've heard that the truth hurts, and it does. The reason the truth hurts is because it allows you to see in a new light the things that made you comfortable in the past. If you're ever in a comfort zone, the minute you're removed from it, no matter your age, you will be uncomfortable. You may feel like there's no need to change. However, I'm going to tell you the truth and let it shift you out of your comfort zone. Let's allow the truth to set you free.

First, I want you to do me a favor. I want you to find the nearest mirror, look in it, and reflect. Reflect on your past. Then we're going to do a project. We're going to label the things that cause you to stay in your comfort zone. What makes you stick with what you know? Is it fear of retaliation or confrontation? Labeling what prevents you from leaving your comfort zone is a huge step toward preparing yourself for change. So, go stand in front of the mirror and tell yourself the truth.

You are staring at a reflection of a beautiful monster. That's what anger has done. Your anger has created the most beautiful, comfortable monster imaginable. Even though God said you're fearfully and wonderfully made, if you don't allow the truth to set you free, you will never see your own beauty. Nobody can see that beauty if you're swinging a fist. Nobody can see that beauty if the hands you're supposed to lift with love challenge others and you become a brawler.

Do you remember the scripture we talked about in chapter one where the woman drives her husband up to the rooftop? If you are a woman who is so angry, violence has become your voice, then no one is going to listen to you. If you have become an "angry black woman," no one will ever see your beauty. Anger will rob you from being the beautiful creature God made you to be. Society won't be able to see anything else, and neither will the man in your life—or your children. Do you realize anger will cause the children you love to fear you? I always say it's better for a child to grow up in a household with one happy, loving parent than two who want to kill each other.

Your family and friends wish you would change. The only way to do that is to let go of your old ways. You have to make a decision that the beautiful person in the mirror is not going to be tainted by the past just because somebody mistreated you.

It is time for you to come out of your comfort zone and face the truth that you have been angry all these years and never knew why. The only way to leave your comfort zone is to shatter the person you've been so comfortable with all these years, the person who made excuses for her anger instead of dealing with the facts.

You might be shocked what your husband, friends, and family say behind your back. They may find it difficult to interact with you or converse, when anger spews out of your mouth like venom from a snake. The only thing you can do right now is accept the truth, and make a change. The only way you can change is to have a good cry and lay your old ways down; it's time for them to die.

You are angry, and we need to figure out why. Let's look in the mirror again and say, "I am angry because _____." Now, fill in the blank and say it out loud. Once you do that, you have to tell yourself the truth, and once you tell yourself the truth, you will be free to be the wonderful, beautiful woman God said you are, and not be harmed by the labels of society.

There's a new you inside you. She's a new you who takes time to smile and give a compliment instead of taking one away. She's a new you who can answer with a soft answer instead of a rage-filled, prideful, and venomous response that causes your entire household or workplace to roll their eyes, suck their teeth, and label you.

That new you is in there, I know she is. Now, the only way to accept this change is to stand in front of the mirror, tell yourself why you are angry, and take twenty-one days to become the new you. It takes twenty-one days to break a habit and twenty-one days for the angry black woman to die. So, you're going to make a list of all the things that have made you angry, and you're going to forgive each one, whether they were your fault or someone else's. Then, once you've told yourself the truth, you're going to embrace the slow death of your comfort zone that you've been waiting for your entire life. Afterwards, it will be time to reintroduce the new you.

CHAPTER THIRTEEN
CHANGE

The biggest obstacle in moving forward is admitting you have a problem. So, say it with me: "I have had a problem with anger." That wasn't so hard, was it?

You may think your anger or bad attitude aren't problems. Many times, when women are told they look angry, they'll say, "That's just the way I look." Well, there's a problem with that! See, that doesn't work with everybody. If you believe that big ball of anger inside isn't affecting you, then there is no need to continue reading this book. Everybody has a little bit of anger that is uncontrollable, but it comes out in different forms.

It's okay. I understand your anger. That's why I wrote this book. You see, I wasn't always a very nice person. I've always been very comical and have always *seemed* like a nice person, but hidden anger affected my relationships.

There's a stereotype in our society that black women are single. For many women, that stereotype becomes a self-fulfilling prophecy. That doesn't have to be you. We've got to detoxify you of your anger so you can coexist with others; the old you did not understand why the anger was there.

Let's bring that anger to the surface, kill that old you, and reprogram you to live a life of freedom. The only way you can be free is to face what has you bound.

The world may say that being a black women with attitude or a whole bunch of swag is a good thing, but it's not. It causes people to look at you like you're a psychopath or call you crazy. And I don't mean a good kind of "life-of-the-party" crazy. I mean the kind of crazy you see in girls on reality shows.

That level of anger and drama makes for great television, but have you ever been watching one of those shows and seen a little bit of yourself? That kind of angry, violent behavior can't exist in a marriage. That behavior can't exist in a friendship, and it definitely can't work in a boardroom or workplace. Have you ever thought about your anger and situations in which you lashed out and then felt ashamed? Did you feel disappointed in yourself?

You know, you don't have to live that way. My mother always said to take the high road, but sometimes that is difficult. So, let me give you something to think about: When you take the high road, there's no room for the low road. You just have to say, "I'm going to express the way

I feel without vulgar language. I'm not going to curse you out, degrade myself, or swing my fists. I'm going to walk away without shame. I've made my point and I'll leave it there for you to think about." If you choose to react in anger, however, you may walk away feeling empty or saying, "There's a better way I could have handled that."

Rage and misplaced anger rob us of the opportunity to take the high road. It's been said that when two fools argue, it's hard to tell who is the smart one. When you allow anger to step forward, you will never be identified as the smart girl in the room.

Anger can give you a reputation. We're here to dispel the rumors about black women, because we're better than that. We're better than what we see on television. We're better than the labels the world puts on us. We're going to show the world that "angry" is not what or who we are. We can get our points across without jumping across tables, scratching, or pulling out each other's hair. We can each find our own men without borrowing someone else's. We will show the world we don't need to be competitive with each other and we've arrived at a place where we can celebrate each other as women.

Each of us has the ability to shift the rumors that surround us if we're just willing to *change*.

❧CHAPTER FOURTEEN❧
NO LOVE, NO SACRIFICE

Boy, oh boy. Here we are, we're almost detoxified. I remember when I decided to do a cleanse, and I was told I couldn't have any sugar. As soon as I heard that, I decided I didn't want to do it, because I'd have to give up something I loved. Well, sometimes in order to change, you have to sacrifice what you love for something greater. Even though I did not want to go without sugar, I decided I was doing myself an injustice by not following the rules.

In order to change, you've got to sacrifice; without sacrifice there really is no love! So, if you love yourself, you have to give some things up. You have to sacrifice that "don't take no crap" reputation. Let go of that name you've made for yourself that has people afraid of you. Lay to rest the fearful rumors that you don't hold your tongue and the attitude that causes people to back away from you.

There's a scripture in the Bible that says, "Do not neglect to show hospitality to strangers, for thereby some have entertained angels unawares," (Hebrews 13:2; ESV). That's another reason you have to watch your bad attitude; you never know who you're interacting with. In order to change, you've got to give something up. Change is good, but it will only work if you allow it to.

In your quiet time, I want you to think about something you might need to give up. Do you have friends who are brawlers? Friends who are dramatic? Friends who are competitive? Friends who are violent?

My mother used to say, "Birds of a feather flock together." Sometimes you have to change your circle before you can change yourself. You have to make a conscious decision and say, "I don't care how much I like it, I'm going to make this sacrifice for me. I'm worthy of so much more. I'm worthy of being loved." A lot of the time, anger prevents us from finding love or being loved, but that doesn't have to be true for you. The greatest sacrifice you can make is for yourself.

Every time you travel by plane they go over safety rules. They always tell you that in the event of a crash, (or any other serious malfunction), an oxygen mask will drop down and you're supposed to place one on yourself before assisting others. Anger prevents you from putting that mask on yourself, let alone anyone else. In your fits of rage, everybody dies! Stop letting that happen. Love yourself enough to know you need to make a change. It's time.

I deal with single women all the time who want to know why they're still single. They ask me, "What am I doing wrong?" If this sounds like you, know it's not that you're doing anything wrong; you've been programmed to believe the angry black woman is right. You rob yourself of the opportunity of loving others. You run people away. So, now that we've revealed why that angry root is there, let's dig it up, burn it, and embrace this beautiful change. Trust me. It can happen.

I remember one time I was sitting in my living room, and I began to think about the change I made when I let go of my anger. It hit me like a ton of bricks. Yes, I'm a wife and a mother, but I haven't always been so nice. Even though I'm a nice person now, I allowed anger to rob me from being a nice person for much of my life. I remember God reaching out and saying to me, "I want you to love your husband, your family, and your children just like I love you."

Oh, that kind of love took sacrifice! The people I surrounded myself with at that time weren't kind people. But I heard God say, "Love them like I love you. I didn't wait for you to get it together, Jameliah. I loved you to a new place, a better place." You know what happened? I sacrificed what I wanted for someone else, because I needed to do it for me. Sacrifice is something you have to do for you. The first sacrifices we're going to lay on our alter are your old ways, your old friends, and your old way of thinking.

❧CHAPTER FIFTEEN❧
THE STRINGS OF UNFORGIVENESS

Pinocchio. Everybody knows his story. Pinocchio was the puppet who sprung to life after a fairy worked her magic and cut his strings. Once he no longer had strings, nothing could control him any longer. He was able to make his own decisions. Most of us have the ability to cut the strings that tie us into controlling relationships.

The twist in this story is that at this point, Pinocchio was more bound than ever. Even though his strings were cut and he was "alive," he had this magical nose that grew every time he told a lie. The only way he could ever become a "real boy," was if he stopped being selfish and stopped lying to himself and others.

And that really is the trick to becoming your true self—you must stop lying and admit your shortcomings if you're ever to be free. Even if you've cut the strings of negativity in your life, you must discover the "real you" and resolve your inner issues, or you will find yourself moving from one type of control to another. Once you find your true self, nobody will ever manipulate you again.

When you don't forgive someone, you are a puppet. When you take the pain of your life, bury it deep down inside, lie and say you're healed, you substitute one string for another. Maybe when you cut the strings of a past relationship, you told yourself you'd no longer be hurt. But your anger continues to surface, and perhaps you lash out at the young man who says, "I can't make it today," and immediately label him a liar. He could genuinely have had something come up and not be able to make it, but deep down in your subconscious you've replaced trust with suspicion. Your defense mechanisms switch on. So, because you don't trust this man, you get defensive. He could just be running late, but you get mad and you lash out, substituting your past experiences and emotions for your current one.

Maybe you keep telling yourself, "I'm free. I'm not mad about that anymore," and yet you know it isn't true. You try to convince yourself that you're free of pain, but you're really not. If your defenses are so heightened, or if you're lying to yourself about how your anger and your past are affecting you, nobody will have a chance to get to know the "real you." Who are you trying to fool?

Baby girl, God sees you, and so does everybody around you. When difficult or triggering situations arise, you get so defensive because you're not free yet. You still have strings and that nose of yours grows each time you lie to yourself. Then, when you get involved in relationships and people say things you don't like, you start yelling and screaming. Or when your kids tell you they "didn't do it," no matter if they're telling the truth or not, you shout. Or when someone's actually being honest, you assume they're lying and get angry because you've been lied to before. You're still angry because you stored those past experiences in your subconscious and said you forgave, but you really didn't.

So, this is what we're going to do today. We're going to cut the strings and we're going to tell the truth. I told you earlier to go look in the mirror, reflect upon those things that are keeping you in your comfort zone, and begin to set yourself free. Now we're going to take it one step further.

You know the feeling when somebody is brutally honest with you and you don't get upset? It's because you don't have strings in that area any longer. When people say things to you and you don't get defensive, it means you have taken control back. So, how do you cut those strings and take control? You forgive.

Forgiveness is nothing but a big, psychological pair of scissors. When you forgive everybody who hurt you, they no longer have strings on you. And furthermore, you don't have to live a lie any longer or bury those seeds of anger and hurt in your subconscious. Forgiveness releases you from living a lie. Then, when things get real, you won't get defensive because you're finally free. You're finally the "real you."

ꙮCHAPTER SIXTEENꙮ
STOP DANCING

By this point, you may have realized that your same old behavior is not working, and it's no longer acceptable. You may have realized that you've been doing the same thing over, and over, and over again, and you may have even found yourself saying, "I'm tired." Maybe you've done some self-analysis, looked in the mirror, discovered where your anger came from in the first place, and decided you're done. Good. You're on the right track.

In Matthew chapter fourteen of the Bible, we learn about Herodias, wife of King Herod, and how she used her daughter to get John the Baptist beheaded. Herodias had her daughter dance for King Herod as a gift for his birthday, which pleased him. King Herod told the young girl she could have anything she wanted, so Herodias prompted her to ask for John's head. King Herod agreed, and had John beheaded. John's head was placed on a silver platter and presented to the girl, who then gave it to her mother.

Women often "dance" for their mothers. They "dance" for their families. They "dance" to make others happy. Although the young girl in this story made the king happy, she only danced to give her mother what she wanted. Nowhere within this story did the mother say, "Thank you," or was she actually pleased; she was simply using her daughter for revenge.

When you watch a woman you love suffer from domestic violence or other kinds of abuse, you find yourself in a place where you say, either, "I'm not going to be like her," or "I'm going to be one up. I'm not going to take certain behavior." But regardless of which choice you make, you're still "dancing" for someone else. You're still "dancing" every time you force yourself to exhibit behaviors that won't make you seem soft, docile, or weak. Even though you've cut the puppet strings and you no longer dance to the beat of their drum, psychologically, you're still dancing. You're still part of the plot and the ploy and the learned behavior you picked up from your past.

It's time to stop. Turn off the music in your head and the voices that say, "Fight back." Get rid of the voices that say, "Lash out," and the ones that say, "If you don't stick up for yourself, then you're just like your mother."

Stop dancing. It's time to do things your way. It's time to say, "I don't need to prove a point. I don't need to do anything to please my mom or anyone else who has an expectation of what strength is supposed to look like." You don't have to put anybody's head on a platter to prove to your mother that you're worthy. Instead, say to yourself, "I'm going to control my own life. I'm not going to allow my mother to control it for me. I'm not going to allow the pain from my past to keep me 'dancing' after all these years."

Maybe you're still angry. Maybe you're still fighting a battle that wasn't even yours to fight in the first place. I always say, "Don't be like your mom, be better." How do you become better? You become better by forgiving. You become better by allowing yourself to live in a healthy way. You become better when you decide that you are no longer going to fight someone else's fight.

If you are still dancing for others, then your dance is in vain. A dance is supposed to be beautiful and allow people to look at you and smile—and possibly dance too. A dance is when you move and act like no one is watching; it is so beautiful, it affects everyone around you. Not only does it become addictive, it becomes a melody where others look at you and say, "Do you need a partner? Let's dance together."

But if you're dancing for the sake of others, you're dancing alone. Nobody wants to dance with you. You're dancing a dance that is so crazy that you're knocking things off the shelf—and you look mad. Your life doesn't look like a dance, it looks like a chaotic mess. The only way to stop dancing for others is to reach a level of self-control where you choose the music, the rhythm, and every step that is made. Get to a place where you don't have to prove your strength and you no longer allow society to pull your strings.

When you work that hard to prove you're "different," you're really just allowing yourself to be controlled. You're allowing people to infiltrate your mind with a dangerous melody that makes you feel tired, misguided, and unloved. No partner is going to tap you on the shoulder and say, "Can I dance with you?" when you are dancing a dance of violence.

It's time for you to stop dancing for others and live your own life. When you do dance, dance to your own music and not your mother's or anybody else's. Don't allow her behavior to infiltrate your life, to dictate your reactions to hostile situations, or to dictate your next move in arguments. Wherever you go, you must display a level of control in your anger.

It is time for you to sit down, take a deep breath, and stop dancing. You are in control of every step, who plays the music, and how you respond to it.

CHAPTER SEVENTEEN

FREE TO LOVE

Your mind has been renewed and you've cleaned out all the old cobwebs that may have caused you to miss out on love in the past. It's amazing how people can be so successful, but fail in their relationships because they just don't understand what they're doing wrong. Well, we've identified that blockage, pulled it to the forefront of your mind, and you've finally identified it and faced it. You've put truth into its rightful place and you're ready now.

You're ready to give yourself the love that was held back for so long. You're ready to reverse your anger and love yourself first, so that you can be there for someone else. Love yourself and say goodbye to the anger that prevented you from being the person you were meant to be, the person God desires you to be.

Anger does nothing. It's like putting a gun to your own head. It's an unspoken suicide that robs you and you don't realize the robber is you. Anger robs you of what you need to have successful relationships in life. It throws up a barricade when someone says something wrong. It makes your defenses so heightened that others can't make mistakes without setting you off. It makes you unable to deal with a person who simply wants to say, "I'm sorry." Anger doesn't allow you to forgive, it doesn't allow you to heal, and it doesn't allow you to live life to its fullest.

But, I have good news. Now that you've identified the source of your anger, you're ready to love yourself. You spent so many years going without, but now you can finally be loved the way you deserve to be. You can have that dinner by yourself sometimes and heal. Or you can spend time with a significant other. Then, when they say the wrong thing, instead of getting angry, you can take a deep breath and think, "They weren't in my past to cause that pain. I'm not going to respond in anger."

Even if you're with someone who says something disrespectful, you can tell yourself, "I'm going to handle this in a way that is so peaceful, God himself would be pleased with my response." This is what the Bible refers to in Proverbs chapter fifteen, verse one when it says, "a soft answer turns away wrath." Wrath is born when anger is repressed to the point that it makes you defensive and you can't respond with a soft answer.

You can give that soft answer now. You can walk out of your house with your head held high saying, "I'm ready." Moving forward, any romantic relationship you may find yourself in will only be a bonus to the self-love you bring to the table. You are ready now, and I am so proud of you for accepting the truth and setting yourself free.

You are now free to love others, and free to love yourself, as well.

ϟCHAPTER EIGHTEENϟ
DISCOVERING SELF-LOVE

You've begun to let go of your anger, and now you're ready to love yourself.

Loving yourself is more than just thinking you're cute or that you look beautiful when you've got a new outfit or hairstyle. It's deeper than that. Loving yourself is about realizing you have a sense of value and self-gratification. Don't get me wrong, that doesn't mean you should be selfish. I'm talking about a love you have for yourself that you can carry into your relationships with others.

You have already taken time to heal from learned behavior, misplaced anger, or anything else that was toxic and may have caused you to become a detriment to your surroundings. You've unmasked the things that prevented you from feeling worthy of love. Now that you've identified the behaviors that prevented you from being successful in relationships, you are free to love yourself, as well.

People who don't realize what love is can't identify it. If they aren't able to look in the mirror and love who they see, they won't recognize love in others, either. Then, when someone with a healthy disposition tries to love them, these people will find that love so strange, or so undeserved, they may even sabotage it.

True self-love is so deep that even if no one else loved you, you would still consider yourself whole. Self-love is not just a feeling, it's an experience—the experience of understanding you are here for a reason and you are worthy. When you enter into a relationship, it is so important to love yourself first, because at that point it's no longer about just you, it's about the other person. If you are so angry that you can't love yourself, nobody else will want to take a chance on loving you. This is why you may find people running the other way, or why it may be hard to maintain a relationship. If you have allowed your attitude to remain violent and angry, you might not even know what love is anymore.

Now that you've removed your delusions and have begun to let go of that anger, you are ready to love. Your brain has been rehabilitated, your mind has been reformed, your thoughts have been repaired, and you are ready to love yourself.

❧CHAPTER NINETEEN❧

I HAVE A NEW NAME

I don't know when society decided that every female's name was "bitch." I don't remember it being on my birth certificate, or on yours, but for some reason, society has decided this is an appropriate name for women. I'm not sure when we incorporated it into our vernacular or began using it as a first name with our last. You certainly wouldn't put "bitch" on your job application, would you? And yet our society continues to accept it.

"Bitch" is not your name, and God help you if somebody calls you an "angry black bitch" moving forward, now that you know who you truly are. There may have been a time in your life when you accepted being called names. If someone said you were an angry black bitch, you may have called them "bitch" right back.

Know this: it is completely unacceptable for someone to address you that way.

The labels of life are now shattered and erased. We are not angry black women and we are definitely not "bitches"—we are just misunderstood. If some women choose to use those words, that's on them. But I'm talking about you. "Angry" is not your name. "Bitch" is not your name.

The Bible says we are fearfully and wonderfully made, and in heaven we will have a new name—not the name our parents gave us. Names have power. You may be identified by what you are called, but you should only respond to what you believe you are. Now that you've detoxified your mind and your heart, your mind is clear to receive the name God has given you.

Our names mean so much to us. Some African tribes and other cultures give names of power. Your parents gave you a name that identified what they thought you were, but you embraced what society said you were going to be. If folks called you "bitch," you probably responded, didn't you? But you have to reject that name. Whether used in an argument or just meant playfully, if someone calls you an unkind name I want you to say, "That is not my name. I am not your 'bitch.' Do not address me that way. I'm a lady and expect to be spoken to as such." Don't even respond to it in an argument. If you are called that name, the argument stops, the disagreement stops.

Say this yourself, "When you call my name, call me by my first name—please and thank you. I am no longer labeled a 'black angry bitch,' or 'bitter bitch.' My name is _____, and God says I'm fearfully and wonderfully made. My name is _____, and I used to be angry, but I am not anymore." You fill in the blank, because now you look in the mirror and you see a totally different person.

We've talked about taking twenty-one days to detoxify your mind of toxic behavior and strife. Using your detoxifying mirror exercise, along with your real name, let's try this whole thing called life again. Let's try again with a new mind, new body, new spirit, and new attitude. You've forgiven your past, so now you're ready to embrace your beautiful future.

Other people's anger does not dictate your life any longer. You have identified the anger that caused others to label you and they have no strings on you. You've stopped dancing and now you realize that you have a whole lot of people to forgive, including yourself. So, you've forgiven the people who hurt you (and you've forgiven yourself) and you realize their fight had nothing to do with you. You're ready to love, and the person you love will love you by your name. They will not label you an "angry black bitch." If someone comes into your life bringing strife and anger, you will tell them you can't be together.

If you disagree with someone, you will do it amicably. You won't yell, scream, holler, or throw stuff to get your point across, no matter who you're interacting with. From now on, expect the people you disagree with to address you the way you address them.

You are a reflection of God. You used to be a reflection of your past, but because you love yourself, you can be reintroduced. You love yourself enough to realize that "bitch" is no longer your name.

ᶘCHAPTER TWENTYᶚ
ANGER-FREE IS THE WAY TO BE

You know how people stand around on New Year's and make all these resolutions about things they're going to do? Or they say what they ain't going to do—yes, I said "ain't"—how much weight they're going to lose, or how much money they're going to save. They make these promises by the strike of twelve. In my culture, they also make chitlins and black-eyed peas, signifying luck and promise. People make all these resolutions, and no sooner than thirty days later, they're back to what they said they were not going to do.

I want you to promise yourself that by the time you get to the end of this book, you are going to live a life free of anger. Promise yourself that you will live a life of joy. Promise yourself that you will be so whole that strife will no longer rule your life. I want you to make these promises, and—here's the important part—I want you to keep them. You can make these promises because a lightbulb has gone off. After examining your life, know that you have been angry for reasons you have the ability to control. You cannot control people's thoughts, actions, deeds, or what they did in the past, but you can control your future, yourself, and what happens moving forward.

The only person who can control the uncontrollable is in heaven. I want you to take what you can control in your hands, and everything you can't, I want you to give to God. This allows you to live a very whole, stress- and strife-free life and only allow people into your life who are on the same page as you. You are no longer in the position where you let anger rule your life, thoughts, vocabulary, hands, or feet. You will no longer allow your life to be controlled by society's issues or people's problems that have nothing to do with you. These are promises you're going to live by, and you can keep them now that you finally have control of yourself.

You have lived every day of your life without control. Being unable to forgive allows you to be controlled by someone else's emotions, thoughts, and actions. Anger and unforgiveness heighten your senses until every little thing that someone does becomes bothersome. You allow yourself to become a raging force and look stupid, foolish, and crazy because you have no self-control. When you forgive, it allows you to cut the strings and to regain control of your life.

I want you to promise yourself today that you are in control of you. You are in control of your hands, feet, mind, thoughts, and actions. If anger makes you lose control, that means you have given someone else the power to control you. So, promise yourself that you will no longer give your power to someone else, no matter who it is. Don't give it to your mother in the past, don't give it to your father (or give it up because you don't have a father), and certainly don't give it to someone who has hurt you or said something wrong. You will no longer let others have control.

You are finally taking your power back by making a promise, an unbreakable promise, that has nothing to do with the stroke of midnight, black-eyed peas, or chitlins. It has everything to do with your willpower to be happy, whole, and free. You love yourself now and you deserve better than this. You love yourself, so how dare you live your life giving someone control to make your emotions go from zero to one hundred with rocket fuel? You love yourself, so how dare you become so uncontrollable that you lose the beauty that God requires you to have as a soft-spoken lady?

Make a promise to yourself, and tell people, "If you think you're coming into my life to bring this drama, I'm sorry. You can't stay. You can't live in my space. It's important and I deserve it, because I robbed myself of happiness for years. I deserve this shot and I'm going to take it. I promised myself that I would love myself and I'm no longer giving you the position to take my power. I take it back. I relabel my life, my mind. I relabel who I am, and I let the world see what anger robbed me of for all these years. I am beautiful, I deserve to be loved, and I'm not angry anymore—anybody. You have no strings on me and I'm free to love myself. I'm free to love me, and I can finally live my life anger-free."

CHAPTER TWENTY-ONE

THE TEST

Okay, now that you've discovered who you are and all the things that kept you bound, the test comes. This is the great test where your faith is challenged and the people you love and call your family and friends begin to challenge everything you have implemented from this book into your life. Understand that as much as we love our families, the Lord chose them for us, we didn't choose them for ourselves. They're not always our friends, but even if we don't always like them, we have to live with them or spend holidays with them. Even though your family may occasionally make you want to throw the mashed potatoes at them, don't.

Now the challenge will come where you close the chapters of this book and incorporate what you have learned into your day-to-day activities— whether it be on the job, walking down the street, or living with someone. We all have people who make our blood pressure go up just by being in the same room. You have to coexist with these people, so you have to put your mind into a new mode of thinking and handling situations. If you think you're going to have a disagreement, walk away. I want you to incorporate everything you read through the chapters of this book with prayer.

I also want you to get a peace buddy. A peace buddy is someone who is going to make you laugh, somebody who knows how to "agree to disagree." Sometimes you have to say, "I disagree with you, and realize neither of us can get our way. We're going to have to agree to disagree." It's important you surround yourself with people who can do that.

You're going to be tested to make sure that old you—the person who had tantrums, threw things, hollered, and screamed—is now gone, dead, and buried. The new you has to show that she has learned how to take a deep breath and say, "Well, I'm not going to come to your pity party," or step back and say, "Well, I'm not going to entertain this argument." The new you is going to use a tactic I like to call the "voicemail ministry." This is when you let toxic people go straight to voicemail. Don't even answer people who you know will want to debate, argue, or spoil your mood. Then—thank God for technology— you can respond via text in a quiet way.

You've got to know how to categorize people when you get to the test. The test is going to be challenging, but I believe in you. I believe you can do it. You owe it to yourself. You robbed yourself of happiness for so many years, and so now when that great test comes, I want you to pass it with flying colors. You're a new person. I believe that while reading the pages of this book, you took a breath and you realized what you were so angry about.

If you meet a person who is angry about your freedom, they're probably just going through the very same thing you just got delivered from. You know how you deal with them? You deal with them by understanding that they are in a dark place, just like you were, where they cannot identify where their anger is coming from, possibly because nobody told them. Just like how hurt people can hurt people, people who are healed want to heal other people; we realize it feels wonderful to be in a place of freedom. I want you to feel the very same thing.

Even though you will want to help others, sometimes they won't understand the new you, they'll try to make a mockery of you, or they'll try to push your buttons. You may even find some people who try to challenge you purely because they want to know if this change is real. They've already labeled you as someone who is angry or causes fights. They already have an expectation of who you are, and they won't believe that you've already reintroduced yourself.

People will come to you trying to start drama, and you're just going to have to walk away. They will be so surprised when you don't react the way they anticipated. Sometimes they may start an argument, expecting you to fight back so they can tell everyone you haven't changed. Don't give them the satisfaction. When you feel that anger creeping back, do an exercise where you smell the roses and blow out the birthday candles. (That means inhale and exhale.) When an argument becomes confrontational, watch your temper monitor. If you feel it rising, walk away. When you realize you are becoming angry, hold your tongue. My mom used to say all the time, "Baby, silence is golden. Honey, you could kill many an army simply by being quiet." People don't know what to attack when you're not saying anything.

Trials are coming and I want you to beat them. I'm already so proud of you. You've gotten to the end of this book, you've done the exercises, and you've identified where the anger came from. You're ready now. You love yourself and realize the worst person in the world you could disappoint is not your mama, it's you. Don't disappoint yourself. Pass the test. Get yourself to a place where you can say to others, "We're going to agree, but sometimes we have to agree to disagree. I don't have to yell and scream and holler, although you may want me to." Even if you slip up a little bit, get back up and continue with your change. When you fall off a horse, the only way to ride is to get back up again. Anything you want to change takes effort. Transformation takes consistency, hard work, and determination, and that means always trying to be better, no matter the situation.

Maybe the holidays are right around the corner. Or maybe somebody's having a party and you've got to visit someone who really doesn't like you. Maybe you get phone calls over and over again from that person in the family who is toxic. Situations like these happen all the time, and these are the people you have to handle differently than before. Now that you've gotten to a different place in your life, you can react in a new way. Maybe you can call a friend instead.

When a person is trying to get free from something like alcohol or drug abuse, they have people who intervene in their lives and create a support system. They have someone they can call when they feel like they've fallen off the wagon. Find your peace buddy. Find your person who, when you feel your anger is going off the chart, you can call and say, "You know I'm detoxifying my life and I need you to make me laugh." Find someone who's got a sense of humor, someone who is going to make you laugh and put you in a better headspace than the one toxic people may push you toward.

Do you remember in school when your teachers would pair you with a buddy so you wouldn't be alone and vulnerable to predators? Get a buddy. You'll go through it together. You're going to pull their coattail and they're going to pull yours. The Bible says, "Iron sharpens iron, and one man sharpens another," (Proverbs 27:17; ESV). Go get your iron. Get someone who's going to say, "Girl, don't you lose your temper, you've been doing so well." Find a support system, someone who's going to rally around you, because you deserve it. You've come so far. The test is coming and you're going to pass it.

When you pass this test and you are a new individual, everyone around you is going to reap the benefits. The new you will bring a peace to your home and your life that you never could have imagined. Do you know who also reaps the benefits of your new personality, your newfound freedom, your new name, and the new you? Your children (if you have them). You have started a new culture in your family and you've cut out the old, negative one. You've broken the generational curse, the learned behavior that has existed in your family for years. You're no longer like your mom, you're no longer part of the whole anger society. You can walk and smell the roses, feed the ducks, take a deep breath, and realize that no matter what comes along, you're finally controlling yourself.

This is a wonderful place to be. There's freedom in understanding that you control your own destiny, because you do! You just may not have realized it before when you were too angry to see it.

Trials are coming. Brace yourself. You've already got the ammunition to fight the war on anger. So, fight it. I've got faith in you. If no one's ever told you they're proud of you, let me be the first: I am proud of you. I'm proud of you because you realized there was a problem and you stood in the mirror and you admitted it. I'm proud of you because you realized something wasn't right for all those years, but now you have identified what that something is and have started making the change. You deserve to have someone say that they are proud of you. You have stopped dancing for your mom or dad and worrying about things that had nothing to do with you.

I am so proud of you!

❧EPILOGUE❧

CLOSING THE CASKET
ON THE OLD ME

At my church, we say something called the benediction; it's the final goodbye before we leave the service. The benediction means it's over. And now that you've pulled things up, cried, wiped your tears, had mic-dropping moments, changed your name, and realized that some things are just not your fault, it's time for us to say "goodbye." You've taken accountability for things you can change, and you'll pray about those you can't.

The Bible says, "If anyone will not receive you or listen to your words, shake off the dust from your feet when you leave that house or town," (Matthew, 10:14, ESV). That is what you've done here—you've moved on. You've shaken the dust off your feet, because it can't go where you're going. You've had self-discovery and you're walking in the newness of life. So, go discover the most amazing life that awaits you. And even if you fall of the bandwagon, you're going to jump back on. You are now determined to say the benediction. You are now determined to watch how everyone responds to your newness.

You can rejoice; you are a new person. You have discovered yourself. You dug deep and pulled up what you needed to. You are worth it. You will "come to terms quickly with your accuser ..." as the Bible says in Matthew chapter five. Resolving your problems quickly means anger can't fester and grow inside of you.

Personally, I've found that after all these years, I can finally say the benediction over my anger issues. I say the benediction over my daddy and I don't blame him, because he was hurt too. I say the benediction over my mother, because she didn't know any better. I say the benediction over anything that caused me pain and made me cry. These things didn't hurt me, they only made me stronger. Now I'm strong enough to realize I'm standing here with all of my glory, knowing it all worked out. Everything in my past was to build who I am right now.

I want you to find an old shoebox. Then, I want you to make a list of everything that made you angry in the past, from your childhood up to last week. Write each of those things on a small piece of paper. Next, I want you to decorate your shoebox to look like a coffin. Color it with black or put black paper on it. Write on the top of the box, "Here lies the old, angry woman." Then, open the box and throw those little pieces of paper in it and say farewell. Say your goodbyes and say aloud, "If I ever have to reach in this box and pull out anything, I will make sure I have mastered it first so it won't affect me."

It's time to say the benediction over everything that caused you pain. You're not going to live another day in your past or in your anger. After you've said the benediction, close the box and stick it up in a closet. Then, shut the door and say, "It's finished. If I should ever lose my temper, I'm going to do it in a way that would please God Himself."

We weren't just mad at our mothers, we were mad at our fathers, as well. But we learned to protect our mothers, and by protecting them, we learned a lesson. That is where we decided we were going to be defenders of ourselves and others. Your defense mechanism was the response to someone else's ignorance and abuse that nearly caused you to ruin your future. But now you know better. The Bible says, "If any of you lacks wisdom, let him ask God, who gives generously to all without reproach, and it will be given him," (James, 1:5, ESV). You have the wisdom to know this wasn't about your daddy, your uncle, your grandpa, your mom, your siblings, your coworker, your ex-boyfriend—it wasn't about anybody who caused you pain. Your issues were due to your tendency to over-compensate for your pain and anger by becoming a raging force when you could have simply grasped control and said, "We ain't doing that. I don't have time for your drama. I'm sorry, I cannot entertain your buffoonery today." Instead, you gathered information and said, "Mommy, I'm going to show you how to fight." And, in defending her, you let go of your best defense: self-control.

So, you're going to say the benediction and close the box. Then you're going to put it up in the closet as a constant reminder of what you have overcome. And when you're mad, you're going to open the box and look at all those pieces of paper that represent your past. You will not put a single one on your back. You will not practice angry behavior, because you've said the benediction. If anybody comes in your life to try to resurrect that dead old soul of yours from the past, they've got to go and you'll have one less egg to fry.

Today you've accepted the truth and you're free to love, live, and laugh. You no longer have to dance, or be defensive over everything. Instead, you're going to smile ten thousand times a day. You've discovered where all the anger came from and you're going to throw it in that box and getting rid of it. You're going to forgive yourself and others, and reintroduce yourself as a newfound individual who is no longer labeled an

"angry black woman." Instead, you are_____.
You are fearfully and wonderfully made, and you
were not intended to hurt yourself or others, or
let anyone else hurt you. Instead, you will stand
up strong and say, "You will not, I shall not, and
we cannot." And, you will do it in a way that is
so tactful, God Himself will smile upon you.

Into the casket goes the angry black woman.
Practice saying this aloud: "Please, allow me to
reintroduce myself. I am and I will always be a
beautiful black woman. I am and I will always be
the type of woman I want my son or daughter to
see. The angry person I was could have caused a
generational curse that would have prevented my
daughter from learning the good, but I am not
going to let that happen.

"Today, I'm breaking the vicious cycle of 'angry
black woman' and I will teach my daughter that
we are ladies. I will teach my son that if he wants
a real lady, he can have one; they're not extinct.
I'm going to teach my children how life can be by
changing the behavior of who I used to be. I love
me enough to give myself a chance. I will say the
benediction and create the life God intended me
to live.

"Farewell. I'm not going to miss the old me,
and I will never resurrect her again.

"Amen."

❧ACKNOWLEDGEMENTS❧

I would like to dedicate this book to my mother, the late Violetta Britton-Young, who taught me strength when my father pulled out my weakness. By both negative and positive working together, I've evolved into this big ball of knowledge used to ignite the world around me. Mom, I am so thankful and honored I had the opportunity to share my life with you and learn all I could. Even though some of the lessons were difficult to swallow, I want to thank you for them. And you were right, all along. I used the tools you gave me to help the world, to change a nation, and to mend hearts. Now, I'm using what God has anointed me to do. As you stated, I've been anointed to do this work and I'm doing it. So, Mom, your lesson was not in vain. I love you more and I thank God you called me "friend." You confided in me, and for this we will forever have our memories and secrets. I'm who I am because of you.

To my dad: I am so sorry you never got a chance to see what God intended me to be. But through you pulling out my weaknesses, I found my strength. I even thank you for every trial and tribulation, for they have made me strong.

I thank you both. Mom, you're my yin and my yang. Dad, you were the energy that allowed it all to work together, because you need the good and the bad to create energy, right? Mom, I love you so much. And Dad, I forgive you.

To my siblings, we may not have always gotten along, but I love you.

Clinton Avenue in Brooklyn, I love you.

My life changed years ago when I discovered true happiness in the arms of two little children, Dylan and Hunter. They have taught me what it is to honor, because I am honored to be their mother. I am honored that God allowed me to have these children, despite every circumstance in my life. It was worth it. I did not know love could be so amazing, but such a headache at the same time! I call you my "Thing One" and "Thing Two." I love you guys more than a thousand pieces of sand on the beach. You could not count that far. That is how deep and unimaginable my love for you guys is. Have I ever let you guys down? No. I promise I won't. I will continue to build an inheritance for you, because you are so worth it.

To my husband, Calvin Wayne Mitchell, I did not know male cheerleaders were better than female! We've always been taught that cheerleaders were female, but oh, if you get a cheerleader who is your husband, you win every game. You are a force that pushes me along with all our children, and Kat Mitchell, I thank you too.

Calvin, I thank you for being with me, encouraging me, and helping me organize. God knew exactly who and what I needed. When the enemy was trying to rip us apart, you helped me stand our ground and we are here. We share our life together and you're going to the grave with me, whether you like it or not. Thank you for your patience.

To my girlfriends, each and every one of you know who you are. You have helped me and picked me up from the ground when I fell. My ladies never judged me, but allowed me to be transparent and never threw stones. I thank my girls for this. I have the best friendships in the world and I love each of you.

My assistant, Deloria Michelle (Moe): Lord God knew I needed help keeping up so he sent me you ... CRAZY LADY, just gansta.

My family, I thank you all. Cousins, nieces, nephews, aunts, and uncles.

To my sisters, we too have some healing to do.

Mark, I thank you for banging on the wall and shutting us up, for laughter was our merry medicine.

CCM, The amazing Car Chronicles Movement family: We have fun every morning at 7:30 a.m.

EST live. I thank you for all of the clicks, tags, and shares. I thank you for allowing me to be part of your morning and really being part of my family.

To my Church, Unity Church Charlotte: I love being your leader, pastor, and friend. Thank you for allowing me to be me.

Now, there is a man I love more than anybody I named. He is a man who goes beyond the human imagination because He is what you call the Alpha and the Omega. He is sweet poetry. He is a song that makes a melody jealous, because it's so sweet. He is the only man who I love more than my husband. I love Him more than I love my children, my family, and my life. He picked me up, this broken girl, shook me off, and said, "Hey, I can use this."

The Lord Jesus Christ. I am here because You took me and You made something beautiful when life tried to crush me. I thank You. Lord, You are amazing to order my footsteps here. I owe you, Lord Jesus, everything.

On the following pages you will find some sample sheets from our upcoming workbook. This workbook is designed to help you work through some of your pain and anger. Check out our website at www.carchronicals.org to sign up for our contact list and we'll let you know when we launch the workbook.

A NOTE TO MYSELF

Dear _____,

I am sorry for:_____
_____
_____
_____
_____
_____
_____
_____.

I forgive myself for:_____
_____
_____
_____
_____
_____
_____
_____.

WORKBOOK

MY PEACE BUDDY IS:

Name: _____

Contact number: _____

Email: _____

I promise to help you keep the peace, signed:

_____

*Blessed are the peacekeepers for they
will be called the children of God.*
—MATTHEW 5:9

WORKBOOK

THE FORGIVING CIRCLE

Gather a group of friends and family once a month with food and fun by starting the Forgiving Circle.

This is a circle to openly speak about forgiving those who offended and hurt you.

The key to the forgiving circle is to confront, heal, forgive, and live.

THE ANGER LIST

Name those you have not forgiven:

1. _____

2. _____

3. _____

4. _____

5. _____

6. _____

7. _____

*But if you do not forgive others their faults
the father will not forgive your sins.*
—MATTHEW 6:15 (NIV)

NOTES

_____

_____

_____

_____

_____

_____

_____

_____

_____

_____

_____

_____

_____

_____

_____

NOTES

NOTES

_____

_____

_____

_____

_____

_____

_____

_____

_____

_____

_____

_____

_____

_____

_____

NOTES

_____

_____

_____

_____

_____

_____

_____

_____

_____

_____

_____

_____

_____

_____

_____

_____

NOTES

NOTES

_____

_____

_____

_____

_____

_____

_____

_____

_____

_____

_____

_____

_____

_____

_____

_____

NOTES

_____

_____

_____

_____

_____

_____

_____

_____

_____

_____

_____

_____

_____

_____

_____

NOTES

_____
_____
_____
_____
_____
_____
_____
_____
_____
_____
_____
_____
_____
_____
_____

CPSIA information can be obtained
at www.ICGtesting.com
Printed in the USA
BVHW070330161118
533263BV00002B/141/P

9 781943 258925